Original title:
The House of Infinite Stories

Copyright © 2025 Creative Arts Management OÜ
All rights reserved.

Author: Adeline Fairfax
ISBN HARDBACK: 978-1-80587-184-2
ISBN PAPERBACK: 978-1-80587-654-0

Whispers in Every Wall

In every crack a secret breathes,
A giggle trapped in dusty cleaves.
They chatter through the night and day,
As walls conspire in their own way.

Old doors creak with tales untold,
Of socks that vanish, and bread that's mold.
The windows wink, the floorboards squeak,
In this land of mischief, nothing's meek.

Echoes from Forgotten Rooms

In corners dark, the echoes roam,
A cat that danced, a ghostly gnome.
They laugh and tumble with the dust,
In every murmur, there's a trust.

Beneath the stairs, a party's cry,
With jests that tickle, oh so spry.
The chandelier sways, a swinging waltz,
As memories giggle, it's never a false.

Tapestries of Time and Memory

Woven bright with threads of jest,
Where silly pasts and future rest.
Each stitch holds laughter in its weave,
And fables funny, they deceive.

The colors swirl, a vibrant scheme,
While hats dance madly in the beam.
Footsteps twirl in the kitchen's chair,
Where spoons have tales beyond compare.

Shadows of Laughter and Tears

In shadows cast by dimming light,
Laughter bounces, taking flight.
Tears of joy in corners hide,
As echoes play, both meek and wide.

The ceiling sways with jests of old,
While tangled wires dare to be bold.
Beneath the moon, they slip and slide,
In this fair ground where secrets bide.

Secrets in the Attic

Under the rafters, dust bunnies play,
Whispering tales of a doggone day.
Bottled-up laughter, behind old doors,
Socks that escape to far-off shores.

A rat in a hat, with a monocle too,
Ponders if cats still think it's taboo.
Old toys are snickering, jesting for fun,
Plotting mischief 'til the day is done.

The Canvas of Living Echoes

Paint drips tales from the wall to the floor,
Where brushes giggle, can't help but explore.
Eras of laughter, splatter and smear,
Whimsical whispers that tickle the ear.

A brush strokes a cat that thinks it's a king,
Paws outstretched, in shared jests they'll sing.
Colors collide in a chuckling dance,
Each hue a joke, a comedic romance.

Rooms Filled with Unspoken Words

Silent corners where secrets conspire,
Lurking in shadows like feline desire.
A couch with a sigh and an old, wise chair,
Chortle in silence, for they can share.

Sticky notes giggle from crammed up drawers,
Trying to spell what the zany adore.
In each crevice, a chuckle to find,
Words left unspoken, but never maligned.

Lanterns of Past Revelations

Lanterns flicker with stories untold,
Casting bright shadows, both warm and bold.
A spoon dances softly, a kettle hums low,
Together they burst into fits of 'ho-ho!'

The clock chimes loudly, a jester at heart,
Ticking and tocking, a comedic part.
Whispers of whimsy cascade from the light,
With every flicker comes giggles at night.

The Parlor of Unfolding Tales

In a room where laughter bubbles,
Every chair has a tale to tell,
The cat wears socks, thinks he's trouble,
As he juggles fish, oh what a swell!

A ghostly friend sings out of tune,
His dance makes the curtains sway,
We peek at stars behind the moon,
As chairs gossip through the day.

Fables etched in Floorboards

Beneath the feet, stories lie,
Of mice with hats and cheese to share,
Every creak a silly sigh,
A rabbit hops, jumps in the air!

The floorboards whisper ancient jokes,
Where bees once hosted a tea affair,
Tickling feet of passing folks,
As spiders weave a tale with flair.

Silhouettes of Those Who Came Before

Shadows dance on walls so bright,
A pirate with a parrot sly,
They plot a cake, a sweet delight,
While the old broom swoops to the sky.

The silhouettes all start to prance,
With hats too big and shoes too small,
In this twist of fate, they twirl and dance,
A misfit banquet for one and all.

A Symphony of Conversations

The teapot whistles, chimes a tune,
While cups dance wildly, almost spill,
The spoons debate who gets the moon,
As forks argue, 'We have the skill!'

A raucous chat of toast and jam,
They break the bread with lots of flair,
While marmalade does a little slam,
In this kitchen, all have their share.

The Path Within

In a hall where odd socks roam,
Lost tales make themselves at home.
Each corner whispers silly tunes,
As cats play chess with wooden spoons.

There's a lamp that only shines at noon,
And a rug that dances to a tune.
Frogs in top hats sip their tea,
Discussing life's great mystery.

Laughter echoes through the air,
Chasing shadows everywhere.
A mirror shows your silly face,
While spiders host a wacky race.

The Storytellers' Sanctuary

In a nook where giggles dwell,
Books spill stories, oh so swell.
A turtle writes a novel slow,
On pancakes topped with maple glow.

The chairs are made of jellybeans,
And windows frame the world's dreams.
A raccoon tells tales of his heist,
While cupcakes giggle, oh so nice.

A clock ticks backward, time goes wild,
As each adult becomes a child.
Laughter bubbles, fills the room,
In a castle built of technicolor bloom.

Chronicles of the Overlooked

Forgotten hats hang on the wall,
They share secrets with the hall.
Dust bunnies hold their meetings here,
Debating if they should disappear.

Old spoons tell tales of stews long past,
As coffee cups hold wisdom vast.
A rubber chicken reigns the floor,
Declaring war on open doors.

Knights of crumpled paper fight,
For a pencil's pure delight.
Time-traveling forks and knives,
Make mealtime the best of lives.

Understanding Through Echoes

Through the walls, the echoes play,
Bouncing back in a quirky way.
Voices mix like a fruit parade,
Bananas talk, and cherries fade.

The echo of a laughing gnome,
Turns lost whispers to a poem.
Rusty hinges sing a song,
While mismatched socks hum along.

A painting's wink admits a lie,
As curtains giggle, whispering why.
In this realm of chuckles vast,
Where echoes make the moments last.

Chronicles Bound in Dust

In a dusty corner, tales reside,
Where socks and shoes have gone to hide.
A cat once wrote a novel or two,
But failed to find a decent boo.

Elders whisper of grocery lists,
That turn into maps of treasure twists.
A lad forgot where he left the pie,
Nowe pigeons feast as a family sigh.

Fiction dances with the silliest lore,
A ghost claims it's his turn to roar.
Between the lines of laughter and jest,
The quiet clock never grants them rest.

So grab a book, and take a peek,
You may just find a talking creek.
Through pages of giggles, don't be shy,
Join the fun, and let your thoughts fly!

Windows to the Unwritten

A window's view might seem quite bland,
But peeking out brings tales unplanned.
The squirrel dressed in a feathered hat,
Plots his grand heist involving a mat.

Rain drops tap a secretive rhyme,
Tiny stories stroll through time.
And what of the dog digging deep?
He's unearthing plots while we sneak peep!

The garden gnome plots a subtle heist,
As flowers chuckle at his odd disguises.
Each gust of wind frames words anew,
What mischief made the morning dew?

In every corner, laughter hides,
With stories fluttering like playful tides.
So open a window, take a chance,
In the unwritten, let whimsy dance!

Shelves of Lost Dreams

On shelves stacked tall, dreams gather dust,
A knight's lost battle with a fearful rust.
A toaster yearns for an epic fight,
With burnt bread crumbling into the night.

An old robot secretly writes poetry,
Confusing lines of blenders' sorcery.
Amongst old shoes and broken toys,
Imagine the laughter of imaginary boys.

Lost dreams whisper in shapes so stout,
Should we open that jar and let them out?
A singing spoon with a sweet serenade,
While a grumpy chair looks for its parade.

Yet as we pull those stories from the dust,
We find new paths, new tales to trust.
In laughter's corner, let's often roam,
For each lost dream could lead us home!

Echoing Footsteps through Hallways

Footsteps echo in cardboard shoes,
As walls chuckle, refuse to snooze.
A secret map under the rug,
Leads to a treasure that's yet to hug.

Whispers trail like cheeky sprights,
Chasing shadows of wild delights.
A mischievous cat with five runners,
Tales of mischief and childish wonders.

Every turn holds a giggling ghost,
Sharing secrets of what they liked most.
Tickling dust comes with tales of old,
Of a brave jellybean dressed bold.

So wander these halls with a laugh in mind,
Discover the stories, one of a kind.
For every echo tells a joke or two,
In the world of tales, there's always a view!

The Alchemy of Time

In corners where the shadows dance,
The clock ticks loud, but takes a chance.
It stops to sip on tea and scones,
While laughing with discarded bones.

A cat with tales of grand old mice,
Swears every room has lived precise.
When windows creak, they share a joke,
Of time that bends and laughs and pokes.

Forgotten hats and old maroons,
Hold secrets from the lazy loons.
They gather dust but come to play,
At midnight's whim, they leap away.

So let us dance through paths untread,
With laughter bright and dreams widespread.
Inside each nook, a jest awaits,
The alchemy our heart creates.

Forgotten Footsteps on Wooden Floors

On wooden floors where giggles hide,
The ghosts of laughter once supplied.
In every creak, a ticklish sigh,
With brooms that sweep the clouds up high.

Forgotten games of tag still play,
Where dust bunnies skedaddle away.
They chase the cats who just won't budge,
While slippers laugh and cozy grudge.

An old cane chair gives sage advice,
It tells of meals and laughs precise.
Each plate a story, each cup a cheer,
As memories swirl through the atmosphere.

So tiptoe down the playful lanes,
Where echoes dance without restrains.
With every step, a chuckle soars,
In realms of joy behind these doors.

The Soundtrack of an Abandoned Room

Dust bunnies dance to the creaky floor,
Old chairs gossip about the time before.
Traces of laughter echo in the walls,
Whispers of socks hiding in closet stalls.

Mice serenade the shadows at midnight,
While shadows play cards under the moonlight.
Lightbulbs flicker like they lost the plot,
In this symphony of what was forgot.

The Layers of Living Histories

Beneath the wallpaper, secrets reside,
Paint peels like layers of a long-lost pride.
Each mark tells tales of a wild old dance,
Some stains reveal more than a mere chance.

The cobwebs hold tales of the timid flies,
As dust motes twirl like they've said their goodbyes.
Who knew a peel could spark so much fun?
Living histories, all tangled as one.

Shelves Heavy with Silenced Voices

Books stacked high like a jumbled dream,
Spilling stories, or so it would seem.
Each spine a whisper, a laugh, a sigh,
Yet they sit quiet while the moths drift by.

Knickknacks chuckle from their dusty shelves,
Knowing secrets even their owner delves.
A teacup with chips tells tales of a feast,
While legends linger of a sassy beast.

The Quilt of Yesteryears

Patchwork memories stitched with a grin,
Faded fabrics where wild stories begin.
Each square is a laugh, a tear, a cheer,
Like patchy old pants, they hold treasures dear.

Grandma's knitting needles click with delight,
As they spin yarns under the soft, dim light.
This quilt of the past keeps the giggles near,
A tapestry woven with every cheer.

Voices Curled in the Corner

In a nook where whispers dwell,
Socks hold secrets none can tell.
Mice debate on cheese affairs,
While spiders spin their tangled flares.

A grumpy cat gives judgment sly,
On tales of birds that dared to fly.
Dust bunnies plot a daring heist,
To nab a crumb, to hold it tight.

A shadow giggles as it peeks,
At awkward chats from ancient weeks.
Each corner sings a playful tune,
Of forgotten dreams beneath the moon.

An Anthology of Hidden Lives

Behind the wallpaper's vibrant hue,
A family of ants hold a barbecue.
The fridge warms up for secret chats,
While leftovers dance with chatting cats.

Beneath the bed, monsters take their breaks,
Plotting pranks and shenanigans in flake.
They joke about the socks they've stole,
And how to hide from a sudden shoal.

In the cupboard, dishes hum and sway,
Retelling their tales from yesterday.
Each plate a hero in its own right,
Daring to dream of being a kite.

The Portrait of a Fleeting Moment

A snapshot of laughter in quicksilver time,
Where toast lands butter-side down every climb.
A wink from a clock that decides to skip,
And a cat that takes all the chairs for a trip.

A tickle of wind through the open door,
Turns crumbs into dancers on the floor.
The curtain sways to an unseen score,
While shadows play games, then ask for more.

The fleeting moment shimmies and grins,
As a toast goes flying, and someone wins.
In this quick blur, the stories unfold,
Where giggles and mishaps become pure gold.

Rhythms of Time's Forgotten Dance

In the attic, clocks tick out of sync,
Each one spinning tales without a wink.
Old shoes decide to start a parade,
While moths and cobwebs throw confetti made.

A couch moonwalks in a clumsy glide,
To grooves of nostalgia it cannot hide.
Books spill their secrets, oh what a sight,
As they leap from the shelf in pure delight.

Teapots tap dance with a tea-stained waltz,
While chairs collaborate in a stunning vault.
Time takes a breather for laughter to rise,
In rhythms forgotten, beneath the skies.

Tales Beneath a Starlit Roof

Once I found a cat with shoes,
He danced beneath the twinkling hues.
A rat applauded with a cheer,
As mice rapped out a tune so near.

A broomstick flew, and off it went,
Chasing tales that twisted, bent.
The walls began to hum and sway,
As laughter echoed night and day.

Grandpa's chair began to chuckle,
While shadows waltzed in playful muckle.
A weasel stole the scene with flair,
And whispered secrets to the air.

With each tale spun, more laughs emerged,
While the moon above gently urged.
Let stories weave through every nook,
For under stars, oh, what a look!

Fragments of the Uncaught

In a cozy nook with books piled high,
A sock puppet claimed it could fly.
It danced on shelves, oh what a sight,
While a goldfish tried to join the flight.

A chicken wandered in with a hat,
Bargaining with the talking cat.
"Let's trade stories, you and I,"
As the goldfish sighed, "Oh my, oh my!"

Then came the ghost, a friend of mine,
Sipping cocoa, feeling fine.
It floated by, making jokes wide,
As jellybeans began to slide.

Snippets of laughter in every crack,
Echoed whispers of tales we lack.
Fragments caught in a whimsical chase,
Under this roof, there's endless space!

The Embrace of Timeworn Memories

A clock struck twelve, but forgot the time,
As turtles raced, oh what a rhyme!
An old sofa chuckled with glee,
While pondering how to brew some tea.

Dust bunnies danced to a jazzy beat,
While lampshades twirled on their little feet.
Grandma's slippers joined the ball,
And tripped over a teddy bear's call.

An attic filled with hats galore,
All claiming to be the tales before.
"Wear me!" shouted a floppy crown,
As a pillow pretended to frown.

Each creak of the floor was a giggling sound,
Of memories that gather all around.
In whispers soft, they fill the night,
While timeworn tales take playful flight.

Guardians of Untold Stories

The oldest book began to snore,
While squirrels plotted by the door.
With acorns stashed in every nook,
They schemed to write their own storybook.

A gnome peeked out from behind a wall,
Holding court with a bouncy ball.
"Who needs heroes when you can play?
Let's turn this night into our day!"

Then came the light, a quirky sprite,
With sparkly shoes and eyes so bright.
"Shall we dance? Or sing a song?
In this realm, you can't go wrong!"

As stories gathered in every fold,
Each guardian grinned, their secrets bold.
With laughter echoing through the air,
Untold stories found everywhere!

Stories that Dance in the Hearthlight

On a rug, tales twirl and sway,
Mice in costumes join the play,
A cat juggles fish with flair,
The fire crackles, tales in the air.

In the corner, shadows prance,
Socks on heads, they start to dance,
A broomstick leads the merry crew,
With giggles echoing, and laughter too.

Chairs hum tunes to every joke,
Walls whisper secrets to the smoke,
The teapot sings, all join the cheer,
In this warm space, no need for fear.

Every corner, a chuckle found,
Every step, a joy unbound,
With every laugh, the night grows bold,
In this bright haven, stories unfold.

The Keeper of Fractured Fables

In a pocket, tales askew,
Wobbly words and penguins in blue,
A giant frog pens puns so bright,
While turtles race in silly fright.

A clock ticks backward, stories rewind,
A bowl of soup with dreams entwined,
The keeper grins, with splashes of ink,
Creating tales that make you think.

Giraffes wear hats; they strut and parade,
In a world where jokes never fade,
Every twist and turn a surprise,
As wisdom comes in the silliest guise.

So grab a chair, don't make a fuss,
Join in the laughter, ride the bus,
For in these fables, joy's the key,
Unlocking smiles for you and me.

Beneath the Roof of Endless Echoes

Underneath, the stories hum,
Cacti dance to a donut drum,
A fish in a hat tells a tall tale,
While snails race fast, leaving a trail.

From the cracks, the laughter spills,
Each word a tickle that gently thrills,
A chandelier made of rubber bands,
Supports a circus of friendly bands.

With echoing giggles, the walls ignite,
Mermaids bounce, a truly odd sight,
A poodle recites, with flair and art,
Each story shared, a laughing heart.

So come and play in this echoing space,
Discover the joys, the funny embrace,
For in the nooks, and beneath the beams,
Lies a treasure of laughter and whimsical dreams.

The Library of Laughter's Ghosts

In dusty shelves where ghosts reside,
Each book a joke, they cannot hide,
An old ghost tries to tell a pun,
But stumbles, leaves us in stitches, spun.

Pages flutter, a gust of cheer,
With silly spirits that persevere,
A phantom librarian, who loves to tease,
Hiding behind the books, so hard to please.

In whispers soft, they tell their jokes,
Of dancing spoons and silly folks,
With every tickle of a turned page,
Laughter echoes through every stage.

So, gather round, the ghostly crew,
For in this library, fun's for you,
Let stories weave their magic, bright,
Turn mundane nights to pure delight.

Song of Dust and Age

In corners where the dust bunnies hop,
The ancient tales just never stop.
A squeaky floor with secrets old,
Echoes the laughter from stories told.

The curtains dance a playful tune,
While shadows glance at the brightening moon.
A sofa that swallows all who dare,
Hides the whispers of a million affairs.

Cobwebs weave in a tangled mess,
Jokes from grandpa leave us in distress.
Light bulbs flicker with silly glee,
As legends float like honey from a bee.

In every nook, hilarity lies,
Wrapped in jest, just like the pies.
So come on in, don't be afraid,
For laughter flourishes in this parade.

Rooms That Hold Remembrance

There's a room with a couch that cuddles tight,
Where the ghosts of high school dramas ignite.
Old photos grinning with cheesy smiles,
Recite their tales in humorous styles.

The kitchen sings of burnt toast fights,
And sticky sweet cake on birthday nights.
Fridge magnets with quotes that amuse,
Remind us of choices we often refuse.

A study where the books have a mind,
They argue for hours, their wisdom blind.
A chair that creaks from stories past,
Says every laugh and tear were a blast.

In the hallway, a mirror's grimace,
Reflects the chaos of our race.
Each room chuckles with friendly glares,
It's a playground for our wildest flares.

Traces of the Untold

Hiding beneath the stairway's bend,
A sock from a game of 'who will send?'
Footprints lead where no one dares,
Whispers of secrets linger in pairs.

The attic holds treasures with a twist,
Dusty hats and a childhood fist.
A rocking chair sways with a grin,
As if it knows where nonsense begins.

In every nook, a giggle sleeps,
Stories of mischief, laughter leaps.
Each old drawer, a riddle awaits,
With socks and spoons and bygone plates.

As a tickle monster roams the hall,
Its laugh echoes, a joyful call.
In the tiniest trace of the bold,
Lie secrets that laugh, never grow old.

All That's Left Behind

In forgotten drawers, a sock mysteriously hides,
Echoing laughter and whimsical slides.
The lost remote plays hide and seek,
While giggles linger on the antique.

A tangle of cords that once had a use,
Whisper of parties with vibrant hues.
Old toys that grumble from their shelf,
Share stories of fun that revive themselves.

Under a rug, a cat's been sleeping,
Dreaming in jests where shadows are leaping.
All that's left behind, a treasure chest,
Filled with laughter, memories blessed.

So join us here, don't rush away,
For jokes are waiting to brighten your day.
In every crumb and creaky sound,
The echoes of joy are always found.

Speaks of Time in Timelessness

In a corner, the clock just yawns,
Ticking slowly through the dawns.
It winks at stories that wait in line,
Poking fun at a world's design.

A cat naps on pages long unread,
While laughter bubbles up instead.
Time trips over its oversized shoe,
Chasing shadows that giggle on cue.

Mirrors reflect what's out of phase,
With echoes of chuckles and silly ways.
Tick-tock's forgotten, it's a fanciful play,
Where moments tease, then run away.

In this realm where nothing's precise,
A hiccup of joy, a roll of dice.
Find funny tales in each little creak,
A universe silly, unique, and sleek.

Rewind and Replay

Press rewind and watch the fun,
To catch the moments chosen to run.
An awkward dance, a misfit phrase,
All play out in comical haze.

The past does a jig, it's all a race,
As bloopers flash with a smiling face.
Dinner dates turn into frosty flights,
While forks fumble in some silly fights.

A beeping machine, hit replay once more,
Where lives twirl and antics soar.
Bubbles of laughter in every twist,
A lighthearted game that can't be missed.

Time's a sketch, a humorous art,
With blunders that tickle, a joyful heart.
Hit pause for a chuckle, then back to the scene,
Where silly tales whisper and gleam.

The Artefact of Lived Moments

A dusty trunk holds laughter bright,
With ticklish memories ready for flight.
Each artifact, a giggle ensued,
From mismatched socks to a fruitless feud.

Socks that danced without a pair,
A rubber chicken, oh what a scare!
Each item a story, quirky and grand,
Where hearts burst open like castles of sand.

Photographs turning red with glee,
Caught in smiles, just wait and see!
Each snapshot whispers, 'What a tease!'
As laughter floats like summer's breeze.

In the corners, old jokes bubble up,
An adventure brewed in a well-worn cup.
Treasures of giggles, mishaps galore,
A chest of stories that beg for more.

Seeds of Stories

Plant a seed, watch it sprout,
Out comes a tale, shouting out loud.
A beanstalk climbs with a grin so bright,
While tomatoes giggle in morning light.

Stories wiggle like worms in the soil,
In a garden where humor's the royal.
Snapdragons chat with daisies all day,
Chasing squirrels who giggle and sway.

Each seed a story that dances and sways,
Like butterflies coaxed into playful plays.
Roots grip tightly, while leaves flap and tease,
Inviting laughter with the greatest of ease.

So come, let us sow, let's lighten the load,
In this garden of giggles, where joy's bestowed.
Each blossom a chuckle, each bud a delight,
Sprinkled with mirth in this whimsical light.

The Sound of Silence Fractured

In a room where laughter starts,
Walls hum tunes, like clattering parts.
Whispers dance without a care,
While cats contemplate their hair.

A clock spins backward, what a sight,
As time flips over, day and night.
Napping gnomes with grins so wide,
Peek at secrets they can't bide.

Frogs on shelves play poker games,
With dice that roll and spark new flames.
Chairs gossip about their wear,
While curtains tease with swaying flair.

The fridge keeps secrets, oh so sweet,
Of snacks that danced on tiny feet.
In this chaos, joy unfolds,
A symphony of stories told.

Enigmas Wrapped in Wallpaper

Wallpaper whispers of old tales,
Of ghosts who wear mismatched nails.
Cupboards laugh and creak with ease,
While socks plot trips to the cheese.

Books on shelves have things to share,
They gossip in a flurry of air.
Mismatched socks with plans divine,
Convene for tea at half-past nine.

A toaster dreams of toasted fame,
While lamps are playing shadow games.
The rugs conspire to trip the toes,
As the fridge dances with tuberose.

Each corner holds a quirky grin,
As mystery unfolds from within.
In this place where oddities stalk,
Each step you take, the walls just talk.

Memories Locked in a Single Room

Inside the box of dusty dreams,
Old hats recall their golden schemes.
Chairs hug each other with delight,
While handles squeak at their own fright.

A dusty record spins a tune,
And spoons plot dances beneath the moon.
Pants debate who wore the best,
While dust bunnies hold a tiny fest.

The window frames a winking sun,
As moths insist they're just for fun.
Toys recall when hands would play,
And wish for just one more crazy day.

This room, a capsule of surprise,
Where memories twirl and capsize.
Through laughter, tears, and tales combined,
Inside these walls, true joy you'll find.

Echoes in the Dust

Dust settles like a sleepy choir,
Each grain a tale of wacky fire.
Old shoes conspire to take a walk,
While doorknobs engage in crackling talk.

The lightbulb winks with a playful glow,
As shadows giggle and sway below.
A broom bears tales of frenzied fights,
That whisk away the dusty nights.

Socks have a union, they plan their escape,
Caught in the washer, all in one shape.
Mirrors chuckle at hidden pouts,
Reflections argue about their bouts.

This dusty realm, a soft surprise,
Where echoes craft their own reprise.
Amidst the mess, joy will be found,
In every laugh that lingers around.

Views from the Attic Window

Atop the stairs I find my seat,
With cats in hats, and mice that cheat.
The world below, a lively play,
While I sip tea and watch all day.

A dog in shades, a squirrel with flair,
A parade of wits, without a care.
I crack a smile as they perform,
In this mad world, I keep warm.

The Spell of Old Documents

Dusty tomes with stories bold,
Whispers of mischief they unfold.
A scroll that dances, a quill that sings,
While paper cats give each other wings.

Recipes for trouble in a jar,
Potions for laughter, they go far.
In ink of joy and gumdrops sweet,
The old spells have a funny beat.

Footnotes of Forgotten Times

Beneath the text, in small print lies,
The tales of socks and mice in ties.
A footnote whispers, 'Here's the jest,'
Of how a bookworm dressed for a fest.

When history winks with a cheeky grin,
And bubblegum laughter makes me spin.
These tiny tales, with giggles entwined,
Remind us all that fun's not blind.

Shadows that Sing

In corners dark, where shadows prance,
They hold a giggly shadow dance.
With ukuleles made of light,
They strum the chords of soft delight.

A shadow's laugh can break the gloom,
As they pirouette around the room.
Their concert sweet, a silly show,
With shadows jiving to and fro.

A Sanctuary of Silent Stories

In a nook where shadows play,
A tale begins to stray.
With knees that squeak and creak,
A truth that's bound to leak.

Each corner holds a laugh,
A spider spun from craft.
The cat with boots on tight,
Pretends he's quite the knight.

A lamp that flickers bright,
Tells jokes both day and night.
The wallpaper peels away,
Whispering what it can't say.

A chair that rocks alone,
Mumbles in monotone.
In this curious place,
Time dances with a grace.

The Attic of Whispers and Wonders.

Upstairs where dust collects,
Time lost, what it reflects.
A trunk of old remains,
Squeaks out the loudest gains.

With hats and shoes piled high,
Each seems to laugh and sigh.
A broomstick takes a ride,
As secrets flip and slide.

The ceiling beams will hum,
With laughter all and some.
The boxes tell tall tales,
Of ships with colorful sails.

An hourglass lost its way,
Sipping tea day by day.
In this attic of glee,
Every corner holds a key.

Whispers in the Walls

Behind the paint, they chatter,
In a gossip bout that matters.
They giggle through the seams,
Sharing all their dreams.

From room to room they sneak,
A platform for the meek.
Their whispers ripple clear,
Turning smiles from a tear.

The pipes hum songs of old,
In a language bold and gold.
While mice tap out the beat,
In this symphony of feasts.

The floors groan with delight,
Poking fun at the night.
Through shadows they gleefully glide,
In this hidden joy, they hide.

Echoes of Forgotten Tales

Beneath the floorboards groan,
Old tales they own.
With echoes soft and sweet,
They bring laughter to our feet.

Caught in a dusty frame,
Each story plays its game.
A ghost with brandy breath,
Hilariously outlived death.

The wind joins in the jest,
Turning quiet into fest.
The window creaks with mirth,
As the moon claims its berth.

Bananas in the pantry,
Could be tales of a banshee!
With every cranny and crack,
The laughter won't hold back.

Chronicles Beneath the Eaves

Under the roof, where shadows meet,
Elves play chess with ants so fleet.
A cat narrates a tale of mice,
While goldfish plot to steal some spice.

In corners, rumors twist and twine,
A ghost writes jokes in sharp design.
The dust bunnies hold a dance-off night,
With squeaks and squeals that feel just right.

Cacti wear hats, and socks are lost,
As grandpa's stories come at cost.
A spoon that sings a song of cheer,
While shadows giggle, drawing near.

Each nook a laugh, each cranny a joke,
Where fortune cookies doubt the spoke.
With giggles soared, we find our fate,
Beneath the eaves, we laugh, not wait.

Pages Adrift in Shadows

In shadowy corners, pages roam,
Whispering secrets of the unknown.
A pen with legs writes silly puns,
While paper planes have funny runs.

The ink spills stories, creating mess,
Of hiccuping frogs who feel no stress.
Scribbles dance like bees in spring,
With every laugh, the light bells ring.

Where books with glasses read aloud,
Jokes about pastries make me proud.
Bookmarks gossip with each other,
Telling tales of Laughing Mother.

In the margins, doodles thrive,
With stick figures looking alive.
As shadows giggle in delight,
Pages adore the silliness of night.

Windows to Woven Dreams

At dawn, the windows yawn and stretch,
With dreams that dance and plots that fetch.
A squirrel in a bowtie steals the scene,
While clouds listen in, oh so keen.

Through glassy panes, laughter takes flight,
As teacups argue 'bout space and height.
The curtains chat in colorful tone,
With stories of kindness, widely blown.

Each view reveals a comic plight,
Where lightheartedness shines so bright.
A curious cat peeks from the ledge,
Musing about leaps over the edge.

Mirrors recall the giggle parade,
As dreams in threads of laughter are laid.
The windows blink, "Come play with us!"
As giggles spark a mighty fuss.

A Tapestry of Timeless Narratives

Woven stories hang like colorful thread,
Tickling the fables that dance in my head.
A tapestry stitched with smiles and play,
Where nonsense reigns, come what may.

With each yarn spun, a mischief is born,
Of woolly sheep who laugh at dawn.
Knitting needles join in the fun,
Chasing their tails, they can't outrun.

In the center, a patch leads the way,
To a world where we chuckle and sway.
A dragon hums, "Why so serious?"
While jokesters gather, oh so mirthful.

Each thread a tale, each knot a laugh,
In this tapestry, joy grows on half.
Where time stands still, and humor strides,
In a whirlwind of light, where glee abides.

Secrets Kept in Wooden Beams

In the beams, whispers creep,
Echoes of secrets that won't sleep.
Naked truth in a squirrel's nest,
A bit of gossip, the very best!

Each nail holds tales of wild delight,
A ghost in the attic taking flight.
Timbers chuckle with every creak,
Sharing laughter, oh so unique!

When the wind hums a mischievous tune,
Hollow sounds bounce, like a cartoon.
Phantom stories dance in the air,
In this place, there's giggles to spare!

Dances of dust in the golden light,
Silly shadows, a comical sight.
Secrets abound in a playful spree,
Nature's jesters, just wait and see!

Laughter Lurking in Hallways

Hallways echo with chuckles and glee,
Footsteps of mischief, who could it be?
A rubber chicken under a bed,
Creaking jokes dance in your head.

Wandering whispers break all the rules,
Knock-knock jokes in the hearts of fools.
Behind each corner, a prankster waits,
With whoopee cushions and friendly mates.

Silly shadows stretching at dusk,
Poking fun, it's a gentle musk.
Tickles of laughter bounce off the walls,
As humor prances and fits in its calls!

With every echo, a memory's born,
A canvas of laughter where spirits adorn.
In this place, no frown shall stay,
Just joy that bubbles in a silly display!

The Attic of Unspoken Lore

In the attic, old hats stacked high,
With tales of adventure, they won't shy.
A mothball's shiver, a sock's retreat,
All twist together, a laughable feat.

Old dolls gossip in a spooky light,
Dreaming of parties gone wild at night.
Rats in the rafters throw a ball,
With tattered curtains that giggle and squall.

Barrels of secrets, a raucous delight,
A treasure of fun hidden out of sight.
Cobwebs weave tales 'til they burst,
In this attic, it's humor we trust.

With dust and shadows that twist and sway,
Every object has something to say.
A chorus of laughter floating above,
In every corner, there's something to love!

Memories trapped in Dusty Corners

In corners where memories softly sleep,
Laughter is buried; it's ours to keep.
A cat with a hat and a grin so wide,
Spills secrets of joy that seem to hide.

Old frames mumble with stories grand,
Puzzles and giggles go hand in hand.
Dust bunnies plot their next big scheme,
In the shadows, they twirl, they gleam!

Jars of giggles line shelves with care,
Unruly adventures float in the air.
With every flicker of light so bright,
Memories beckon, sparking delight!

So here in the corners, we'll share our tales,
Spun with humor, where laughter prevails.
With each chuckle, the world feels right,
In dusty nooks, joy takes flight!

Portraits of Lives Unlived

In frames of dust, they grin so wide,
Each one a tale that took a ride,
A pirate's hat on a banker's head,
Who knew a fortune could be misled?

A chef who dreams of flights and sails,
In kitchens, he cooks up ninja tales,
He's hunted by spoons, in a culinaire spree,
Ah, just one bite and he could fly free!

An artist paints with jelly beans,
Colorful worlds from silly scenes,
A castle made of bubblegum,
Each wall a tale, and yum, yum, yum!

So here they sit, in quiet laughter,
Funny lives filled with absurd chapters,
A dance in dreams that can't be still,
In the gallery where whims fulfill.

Stairs that Lead to Yesterdays

Up the stairs where squeaks reside,
A pair of socks that left the ride,
They tell of trips on rainbow skies,
With jellyfish and gymnastic pies.

Each step a memory, each creak a song,
A monkey's tune that feels so wrong,
A dance-off with a shy old cat,
In the attic where all stories chat.

The pendulum swings, tick and tock,
Time's a jester, dressed as a clock,
It trips and slips, a playful tease,
Waltzing on floors that laugh with ease.

And if you listen closely, my friend,
You might hear the laughter never ends,
For stairs are stories, some bold, some shy,
Just hold on tight, as dreams pass by.

Forgotten Corners of the Heart

In a nook where dust bunnies cling,
Forgotten dreams begin to sing,
A mismatched sock with a quirky grin,
Tales of dance-offs it could win.

A teapot hums from days long gone,
Its whistling tune a playful song,
It bleats of tea parties with no guests,
Where laughter swirls and joy invests.

Old shoes are hiding, covered in twirl,
With stories spun in a dance-like whirl,
They've walked through puddles of jellyfish gold,
In forgotten corners, legends unfold.

So tiptoe in softly, let life impart,
The giggles and chuckles of a beating heart,
For all the silly dreams we hold dear,
Are waiting right here, so never fear.

The Whirlwind of Words

Words fly about like bees in spring,
Some are jesters, while others sing,
A pun here, a joke there,
In the whirlwind, they toss and flare.

A hiccup of laughter, a flash of grace,
Words trip in a most chaotic race,
They tangle and twist, a conga line,
Forming a dance that's simply divine.

With riddle and ruckus, they play their games,
A word wizard stirs up funny names,
The salad speaks, the cookie crumbs,
In this wild world, absurdity hums.

So grab a phrase, give it a whirl,
In the whirlwind of words, let your mind unfurl,
For every chuckle, every little cheer,
Is a giggle we savor throughout the year.

Echoes beneath the Timbers

In a room where laughter lingers,
Echoes dance on creaky floors,
A cat plots with swinging fingers,
And knocks down books by scores.

Each tome a tale of mishap,
As ghosts giggle in their sleep,
A pirate takes a map nap,
While chickens in the library peep.

A knight's armor starts to shimmy,
When tickled by a passing breeze,
Oh look, it's not even Jimmy,
But a squirrel searching for cheese.

So gather 'round with eager ears,
As the walls start to share their glee,
With stories that tickle your fears,
And chase dreams up a tallsy tree.

The Wind's Tale through Open Windows

The wind whispers secrets so sly,
Through windows wide and cheerful,
It tells of a frog who can fly,
Wearing socks that are truly fearful.

A raccoon in a top hat struts,
Claiming it's his best attire,
While trying to dance in a rut,
And whimsically misfires.

Polka-dots clash with stripes galore,
As laughter sweeps through the air,
A wild parade at the door,
Brings tales that prompt a stare.

So let the breeze carry you far,
To worlds where nonsense reigns,
Where every twinkling star,
Bears witness to these whimsical chains.

Flickering Stories in Candlelight

Candle flames play peek-a-boo,
Casting shadows of a mime,
Who drops his hat and takes a cue,
To dance with the toes of time.

Between the flickers, secrets spin,
Of owls that cook in the night,
A goat who can slyly grin,
While juggling pastries, what a sight!

The mice hold a grand debate,
On cheese that sings or just hums,
While telling tales of a fortunate fate,
Where laughter and mischief comes.

So sit back, let the stories unfold,
In warm, dancing glow delight,
For in each twist, humor holds,
A universe brought to light.

Paths of Pen and Paper

With a quill that dances about,
Tales leap onto the page,
A dragon with a silly pout,
Is caught in a rhyming cage.

A fish that dreams of becoming,
A rock star in a flashy dress,
Swoons as it's dramatically strumming,
While readers giggle and express.

Ninja turtles and silly kings,
Fight over who wears the crown,
While flying cats cheer and sing,
As silly chaos goes down.

So let ink flow like a stream,
Where laughter finds its way,
In this whimsical, funny dream,
Where stories dance and play.

Weaving Whimsy into Walls

In a room where shadows dance,
Giggles hide in every glance.
Pictures chatter on the walls,
As socks debate their missing calls.

Chairs hold court with squeaky tales,
While curtains plot their windy gales.
A clock tick-tocks with cheeky glee,
Whispering secrets, just to me.

Lampshades sway in laughter's light,
Painting dreams throughout the night.
A rug tells jokes from days of yore,
And slippers sneak to the fun galore.

In this space where whimsy reigns,
Tales of silliness break the chains.
Beneath the roof where jesters dwell,
The stories rise and twist so well.

The Heartbeat of Forgotten Legends

In a nook where old tales breathe,
The fridge hums softly, like a wreath.
Ghosts of pastries long since baked,
Have crumbs of laughter still awake.

Books stand tall, with dusty spines,
Whispering plots of silly signs.
A spoon recalls the minty pie,
While squeaky doors sing lullabies.

Under beds, the dust bunnies play,
Hosting dances at end of day.
The calendar flirts with days gone past,
Where every moment wears a mask.

Legends linger in pots and pans,
With stories spun by playful hands.
Here time winks, it never frets,
Turning whimsy into sweet debts.

Corners where Memories Reside

In the corners, laughter lingers,
Tickling toes with clever fingers.
Behind the couch, a sock peers out,
With a grin, it whispers, no doubt.

Dust claws at the seams of fate,
While lost buttons speculate.
A blanket fort, a dreamer's lair,
Cradles whims beyond compare.

Underneath the table's fold,
A treasure trove of stories told.
Crayons hum their colorful tunes,
In quiet corners, they chase the moons.

Here shadows hide, but dreams don't flee,
Every creak, a burst of glee.
Each corner blooms with echoes bright,
Celebrating the delightful night.

Bridges of Thoughts Unspoken

Between the beams where laughter lingers,
Ideas sway with eager fingers.
Cupcakes giggle in the pantry light,
Handing out wishes on a flight.

The walls whisper in playful tones,
While echoes chase the drowsy moans.
A table for chit-chat keeps,
Dreams wrapped tight in pudding heaps.

Socks often wander far and wide,
Searching humor as their guide.
Each creak, each pop, a friendly nudge,
Inviting tales that won't budge.

Bridges twist with laughter's sound,
Connecting hearts that spin around.
In this space, where echoes gleam,
Thoughts unspoken form the theme.

Time's Tattered Manuscript

In a corner a tome, all tattered and torn,
Its pages are giggles, and prose that's worn.
The plots run in circles, like a cat chasing feet,
Where characters tripped over their own two left feet.

A knight who is scared of a ladybug's sting,
A dragon who dances, he's quite the king.
The stories get stuck in a wild, silly dance,
And every sweet chapter gives laughter a chance.

A wizard who sneezes, then turns into cheese,
While fairies in socks bounce around with ease.
Each line's a riddle, a whimsical scheme,
In this storybook where nothing's as it seems.

The Garden of Forgotten Whispers

In a garden where giggles grow taller than trees,
Hidden jokes blossom in a flurry of breeze.
A scarecrow is chuckling at puns in the air,
While gnomes make pacts with their wisecracking hair.

The flowers gossip, in colors so bright,
About beetles who dance under moonlight delight.
A parrot insists that it knows all the jokes,
While rabbits tell tales of their bumbles and pokes.

The pond always ripples with laughter so sweet,
As frogs wear top hats and tap dance their beat.
This garden of whispers, a whimsical land,
Where stories take root, and dreams oft expand.

Ghosts of Laughter and Sorrow

In the attic they linger, these phantoms of cheer,
Telling tales of the blunders from yesteryear.
A specter who snickers at secrets long past,
With echoes of laughter that forever will last.

The ghost of old Tim, with a cobwebby wail,
Swears he can juggle with a banana fish tail.
While witches brew tea made of giggles and sighs,
And humor creeps out with the dawn 'neath the skies.

Though shadows might linger, they dance in delight,
Spinning tales of sorrow that sparkle so bright.
In this haunt of humor, where ghouls take a bow,
They'll turn grief to laughter, if only you allow.

Dreams Dusted on the Shelves

On the shelves of the mind, where stories stack high,
Dreams dusted gently with a wink and a sigh.
A treasure trove twinkling, of nonsense out loud,
In the corners where giggles tend to feel proud.

Each book a wild journey, a trip to the moon,
Where raccoons wear tutus and dance to a tune.
With crayons for pencils, and laughter for ink,
These tales tell of mishaps we couldn't outthink.

A fable of socks that mysteriously flee,
While kittens debate on what next they should see.
In this cacophony of jest and delight,
These dreams are the magic that twinkle each night.

The Fabric of Fleeting Memories

In corners where laughter clings,
Sock puppets dance and do strange things,
Old photos giggle, tales they spin,
A cat in a hat, oh where to begin?

Time takes a tumble, flips like a coin,
A chattering chair does point and join,
The quilt of the past threads silly and bright,
A prince made of pudding taking flight!

In forgotten nooks, odd socks convene,
Creating a circus that's rarely seen,
The echoes of giggles paint shadows wide,
As our buddy the broom gives a starry ride!

So here in this parlor of glimmer and fun,
Memories twirl, like a dance never done,
With tickles of time in fabric and glee,
Life's hiccuping moments keep calling to me.

A Journey Through Echoing Doors

Behind every door, a riddle awaits,
A sock and a shoe debate their fates,
Upon a grand staircase, a duck takes a leap,
While a whispering broom helps secrets to keep.

Through corridors painted with laughter and cheer,
A mouse on a skateboard zooms in from the rear,
The doorknobs giggle, they twist and they turn,
Each entry a prank, with lessons to learn.

With each creak and squeak, the room's full of zest,
A carousel of oddities, put to the test,
A fountain of stories, each splash comes alive,
In the wild wit of whimsy, the tales we derive.

So wander these halls, each doorway's a gift,
With echoes that wiggle, and voices that lift,
Here's to the quirky, the silly, the dare,
For every sweet journey holds laughter to share.

Spinning Tales at Twilight

As the sun dips low, whirligigs whirl,
A dragon made of noodles begins to twirl,
With shadows that chuckle and then start to play,
They weave in and out as the skies turn gray.

At twilight's embrace, the fireflies hum,
A roast on the griddle prepares to run,
Fish fly through the air, with a wink and a splash,
While reality bends in a hilarious clash.

A tree swings its branches, whispering jokes,
The moon beams down, joins in with the pokes,
Old tales get tangled in giggles and grins,
As twilight spins yarns for the wild-hearted wins.

So gather 'round fires, let silliness reign,
Where stories unfold like a light summer rain,
In the glow of the night, with laughter untamed,
We breathe in the magic, all shadows proclaimed.

When Walls Remember

These walls have ears and a sneaky grin,
They murmur the tales of where we've been,
A ghost of a hiccup caught on every beam,
Tickling the heart with an echoing dream.

While secret compartments break into cheer,
A banana peel slips—yes, that's quite near,
Divas of dust bunnies sway on their toes,
As echoes of laughter through every crack flows.

Down dusty hallways with mischief abounds,
Old slippers in disco, spinning round and around,
The walls share their secrets in whispers so light,
Each crack a reminder of sheer delight.

So listen close now, let memory sing,
For every odd wall has a story to fling,
In the heart of the home where humor takes flight,
The walls remember it all, day and night.

Fabric of the Unseen Clutch

In corners where the shadows play,
A sock steals time, but where's the way?
A family of shoes, they argue in pairs,
Arguing whose stench is worse, but no one cares.

The cat sits proud atop a hat,
Plans a heist involving the neighbor's mat.
While dust bunnies dance a jolly old jig,
Creating a whirlpool from a well-fed twig.

Each drawer holds secrets, a sacred trust,
From grandma's teeth to a spoonful of rust.
A pickle jar filled with forgotten receipts,
They laugh at our spending and all our defeats.

In fabric where laughter's tightly sewn,
The mysteries hum in a whimsical tone.
So grab a cup, let stories unfurl,
In this quirky realm, we spin and swirl.

Murmurs from the Cellar Depths

Echoes of laughter creep from below,
A vegetable orchestra begins the show.
Tomatoes croon while onions do waltz,
Each one insists, 'It's not my fault!'

Mice gather round for the grand feast,
Nibbling on cheese, they're quite the beast.
They spin tales of cats who dare to nap,
Swishing their tails in a daring trap.

Old bottles chuckle, half-filled with cheer,
Whispering secrets that no one can hear.
A ghost of a soup pot stirs up a plot,
To vanish the recipes, left to rot.

So come on down, heed the call,
In cellar's embrace, you might just fall.
With giggles and gasps, tales will unfold,
In the murk and the magic, watch stories be told.

Tales Unfolding in the Rain

Raindrops gather like old friends tight,
Sharing stories from morning till night.
Umbrellas dance in a wobbly line,
Each bounces along, claiming, 'This rain's fine!'

Puddles become stages for frogs on the hop,
Ballet of the braves, they twirl and plop.
The trees sway and giggle, their branches all drip,
While squirrels in hats sail a leaf on a trip.

The streets become rivers of storytelling delight,
While passersby slip and squeak with fright.
Who knew that the rain could have such a laugh?
Mama ducks quip, "It's a perfect gaffe!"

So grab your boots, let imagination reign,
Find joy in the downpour, let go of the pain.
For every drop carries a hint of a joke,
In this laughing downpour, we all feel woke.

The Lantern of Lost Chronicles

In attics dusty and worn, tales flare,
A lantern flickers, showing what's rare.
Forgotten books gathered, wear tales like gold,
Spinning yarns of a cat that danced bold.

A birthday cake left out, still intact,
Candles are snickering, posing with tact.
The spatulas whisper of baking gone wrong,
While mixing bowls hum a sweet, silly song.

Pictures awaken and jump from the frames,
Reliving the moments, recalling the names.
A broom winks slyly, ready to sweep,
With all of its friends for a giggly heap.

So come, light the lantern, and just let it spin,
For every lost story wants a friend's grin.
In this world of wonder, come take a peek,
Where characters frolic and laughter's not weak.

Staircases to Forgotten Realms

Up the stairs, a silly cat,
Wearing a hat that's far too fat.
He tripped and tumbled, what a sight,
Landed in books, oh what a fright!

Each step holds a giggle, a cheer,
Whispered tales we long to hear.
From dragons dancing, to frogs on stilts,
A world of nonsense, laughter built.

At the top, a door creaks wide,
A wacky world sits inside.
Clouds of cake and rivers of juice,
Where every laugh is now let loose!

So grab a tale, take a leap,
Where even shadows play and peep.
Each journey's fun, a laugh-filled spree,
In realms of wonder, wild and free!

The Library of Endless Tomorrows

In the library, a parrot talks,
With jokes that make the old clock squawk.
It tells of wizards tripping on feet,
And wands that never taste defeat.

Librarians dance in their towering hats,
Chasing bookworms, and playful brats.
Each shelf a stage for ripe delight,
Where every page twists into flight.

Tomorrow's tales are shaped today,
In wiggly words that tease and play.
A dragon's sneeze, a giant's shoes,
Adventures brew in wildly hues.

So wander through, with smiles bright,
In this whimsical bookish light.
For laughter echoes off each wall,
In this merry library, we have a ball!

Gables of Hidden Narratives

Up in the gables, stories creep,
Where squirrels giggle and hedgehogs leap.
Each window holds a mischievous grin,
As tales of oddities quietly spin.

There's a tap-dancing mouse with flair,
And socks for hats, beyond compare.
They waltz through chapters, twirling by,
As whispers of mischief flutter and fly.

Under the eaves, a fox recites,
Absurd adventures under moonlight nights.
Puns that stretch like the very sky,
Each twist and turn makes laughter sigh.

So peek inside, join the fun,
Where laughter's puzzle has just begun.
In gables echoing with stories untold,
A whimsical world awaits, bold and gold!

Portraits of Lives Long Gone

In the gallery, the portraits grin,
With mustaches twirling, where to begin?
A lady winks with a jolly air,
Her pet pig in a dapper chair.

Sir Lancelot trips on his own lance,
As knights in armor join the dance.
Each frame a joke from yesteryears,
With echoes of laughter and silly cheers.

A jester bows with a silly face,
In every portrait, a funny place.
Their antics chase away the gloom,
While colors swirl in the crowded room.

So let's raise a toast to the past,
With giggling faces that forever last.
For every tale captured on a wall,
Is a memory wrapped in a hearty call!

www.ingramcontent.com/pod-product-compliance
Lightning Source LLC
Chambersburg PA
CBHW070007300426
43661CB00141B/297